PLEASE RETURN

REWARD FOR RETURN:

Inside the pages of this journal you will find seven types of pages: Prayer Requests, Answered Requests, Prayers for Salvation, Families of the Church, Community Families, Community Schools, and Community Organizations.

Because God's ways and timing are different than ours, our prayers will not always be answered immediately or in the way you would have them work out.

You can link the Prayer Requests by numbering or adding symbols to the grey box on the request line with the corresponding line on Answered Requests line.

I pray God does more than you could ask or imagine as you present your requests to Him.

Reverend Eric Sanford

DO NOT BE ANXIOUS ABOUT ANYTHING, BUT IN EVERY SITUATION, BY PRAYER AND PETITION, WITH THANKSGIVING, PRESENT YOUR REQUESTS TO GOD. AND THE PEACE OF GOD, WHICH TRANSCENDS ALL UNDERSTANDING, WILL GUARD YOUR HEARTS AND YOUR MINDS IN CHRIST JESUS.

PHILIPPIANS 4:6-7

A Pastor's Prayer Journal
Parish Edition

Pastor, God has called you to tend the spiritual needs of your entire community.

A Pastor's Prayer Journal-The Parish Edition includes specific ways to pray for the community where God has called you to serve Him.

Communities are made up of families, organizations and businesses, and schools.

As you connect with families, organizations, and schools bring them before the Lord and pray for the good of all in your parish, city, neighborhood, or community.

> THUS SAYS THE LORD OF HOSTS, THE GOD OF ISRAEL, TO ALL THE EXILES WHOM I HAVE SENT INTO EXILE FROM JERUSALEM TO BABYLON: 5 BUILD HOUSES AND LIVE IN THEM; PLANT GARDENS AND EAT THEIR PRODUCE. 6 TAKE WIVES AND HAVE SONS AND DAUGHTERS; TAKE WIVES FOR YOUR SONS, AND GIVE YOUR DAUGHTERS IN MARRIAGE, THAT THEY MAY BEAR SONS AND DAUGHTERS; MULTIPLY THERE, AND DO NOT DECREASE. 7 BUT SEEK THE WELFARE OF THE CITY WHERE I HAVE SENT YOU INTO EXILE, AND PRAY TO THE LORD ON ITS BEHALF, FOR IN ITS WELFARE YOU WILL FIND YOUR WELFARE.
>
> JEREMIAH 29:4–7

PRAYER REQUESTS

DATE	PRAYER	ANSWER

PRAYER REQUESTS

DATE	PRAYER	ANSWER

PRAYER REQUESTS

DATE	PRAYER	ANSWER

PRAYER REQUESTS

DATE	PRAYER	ANSWER

PRAYER REQUESTS

DATE	PRAYER	ANSWER

PRAYER REQUESTS

DATE	PRAYER	ANSWER

PRAYER REQUESTS

DATE	PRAYER	ANSWER

PRAYER REQUESTS

DATE PRAYER ANSWER

PRAYER REQUESTS

DATE	PRAYER	ANSWER

PRAYER REQUESTS

DATE	PRAYER	ANSWER

PRAYER REQUESTS

DATE	PRAYER	ANSWER

PRAYER REQUESTS

DATE	PRAYER	ANSWER

PRAYER REQUESTS

DATE	PRAYER	ANSWER

PRAYER REQUESTS

DATE	PRAYER	ANSWER

PRAYER REQUESTS

DATE	PRAYER	ANSWER

PRAYER REQUESTS

DATE	PRAYER	ANSWER

PRAYER REQUESTS

DATE	PRAYER	ANSWER

PRAYER REQUESTS

DATE	PRAYER	ANSWER

PRAYER REQUESTS

DATE	PRAYER	ANSWER

PRAYER REQUESTS

DATE	PRAYER	ANSWER

PRAYER REQUESTS

DATE	PRAYER	ANSWER

PRAYER REQUESTS

DATE	PRAYER	ANSWER

PRAYER REQUESTS

DATE	PRAYER	ANSWER

PRAYER REQUESTS

DATE	PRAYER	ANSWER

PRAYER REQUESTS

DATE	PRAYER	ANSWER

PRAYER REQUESTS

DATE PRAYER ANSWER

PRAYER REQUESTS

DATE	PRAYER	ANSWER

PRAYER REQUESTS

DATE PRAYER ANSWER

PRAYER REQUESTS

DATE	PRAYER	ANSWER

PRAYER REQUESTS

DATE	PRAYER	ANSWER

PRAYER REQUESTS

DATE	PRAYER	ANSWER

PRAYER REQUESTS

DATE	PRAYER	ANSWER

PRAYER REQUESTS

DATE PRAYER ANSWER

PRAYER REQUESTS

DATE	PRAYER	ANSWER

PRAYER REQUESTS

DATE	PRAYER	ANSWER

PRAYER REQUESTS

DATE	PRAYER	ANSWER

PRAYER REQUESTS

DATE	PRAYER	ANSWER

PRAYER REQUESTS

DATE	PRAYER	ANSWER

PRAYER REQUESTS

DATE PRAYER ANSWER

PRAYER REQUESTS

DATE	PRAYER	ANSWER

PRAYER REQUESTS

DATE	PRAYER	ANSWER

PRAYER REQUESTS

DATE	PRAYER	ANSWER

PRAYER REQUESTS

DATE	PRAYER	ANSWER

PRAYER REQUESTS

DATE PRAYER ANSWER

PRAYER REQUESTS

DATE PRAYER ANSWER

PRAYER REQUESTS

DATE	PRAYER	ANSWER

PRAYER REQUESTS

DATE	PRAYER	ANSWER

PRAYER REQUESTS

DATE	PRAYER	ANSWER

PRAYER REQUESTS

DATE	PRAYER	ANSWER

PRAYER REQUESTS

DATE	PRAYER	ANSWER

PRAYER REQUESTS

DATE PRAYER ANSWER

PRAYER REQUESTS

DATE	PRAYER	ANSWER

PRAYER REQUESTS

DATE	PRAYER	ANSWER

PRAYER REQUESTS

DATE	PRAYER	ANSWER

PRAYER REQUESTS

DATE	PRAYER	ANSWER

PRAYER REQUESTS

DATE	PRAYER	ANSWER

PRAYER REQUESTS

DATE	PRAYER	ANSWER

PRAYER REQUESTS

DATE	PRAYER	ANSWER

PRAYER REQUESTS

DATE	PRAYER	ANSWER

PRAYER REQUESTS

DATE	PRAYER	ANSWER

PRAYER REQUESTS

DATE	PRAYER	ANSWER

PRAYER REQUESTS

DATE	PRAYER	ANSWER

ANSWERED REQUESTS

DATE ANSWER

ANSWERED REQUESTS

DATE ANSWER

ANSWERED REQUESTS

DATE ANSWER

ANSWERED REQUESTS

DATE ANSWER

ANSWERED REQUESTS

DATE ANSWER

ANSWERED REQUESTS

DATE	ANSWER

ANSWERED REQUESTS

DATE	ANSWER

ANSWERED REQUESTS

DATE	ANSWER

ANSWERED REQUESTS

DATE ANSWER

ANSWERED REQUESTS

DATE ANSWER

ANSWERED REQUESTS

DATE ANSWER

ANSWERED REQUESTS

DATE ANSWER

ANSWERED REQUESTS

DATE ANSWER

ANSWERED REQUESTS

DATE	ANSWER

ANSWERED REQUESTS

DATE ANSWER

ANSWERED REQUESTS

DATE ANSWER

ANSWERED REQUESTS

DATE ANSWER

ANSWERED REQUESTS

DATE ANSWER

ANSWERED REQUESTS

DATE ANSWER

ANSWERED REQUESTS

DATE ANSWER

ANSWERED REQUESTS

DATE ANSWER

ANSWERED REQUESTS

DATE ANSWER

ANSWERED REQUESTS

DATE ANSWER

ANSWERED REQUESTS

DATE ANSWER

ANSWERED REQUESTS

DATE ANSWER

ANSWERED REQUESTS

DATE ANSWER

ANSWERED REQUESTS

DATE ANSWER

ANSWERED REQUESTS

DATE ANSWER

ANSWERED REQUESTS

DATE ANSWER

ANSWERED REQUESTS

DATE	ANSWER

ANSWERED REQUESTS

DATE ANSWER

ANSWERED REQUESTS

DATE ANSWER

ANSWERED REQUESTS

DATE ANSWER

ANSWERED REQUESTS

DATE ANSWER

PRAYER FOR SALVATION

DATE	PERSON	DETAILS

PRAYER FOR SALVATION

DATE PERSON DETAILS

PRAYER FOR SALVATION

DATE PERSON DETAILS

PRAYER FOR SALVATION

DATE	PERSON	DETAILS

PRAYER FOR SALVATION

DATE PERSON DETAILS

PRAYER FOR SALVATION

DATE	PERSON	DETAILS

PRAYER FOR SALVATION

DATE PERSON DETAILS

PRAYER FOR SALVATION

DATE	PERSON	DETAILS

PRAYER FOR SALVATION

DATE	PERSON	DETAILS

PRAYER FOR SALVATION

DATE	PERSON	DETAILS

FAMILIES OF THE CHURCH

DATE	FAMILY	PRAYER

FAMILIES OF THE CHURCH

DATE	FAMILY	PRAYER

FAMILIES OF THE CHURCH

DATE FAMILY PRAYER

FAMILIES OF THE CHURCH

DATE FAMILY PRAYER

FAMILIES OF THE CHURCH

DATE	FAMILY	PRAYER

FAMILIES OF THE CHURCH

DATE	FAMILY	PRAYER

FAMILIES OF THE CHURCH

DATE	FAMILY	PRAYER

FAMILIES OF THE CHURCH

DATE	FAMILY	PRAYER

FAMILIES OF THE CHURCH

DATE	FAMILY	PRAYER

FAMILIES OF THE CHURCH

DATE	FAMILY	PRAYER

COMMUNITY FAMILIES

DATE	FAMILY	PRAYER

COMMUNITY FAMILIES

DATE	FAMILY	PRAYER

COMMUNITY FAMILIES

DATE	FAMILY	PRAYER

COMMUNITY FAMILIES

DATE	FAMILY	PRAYER

COMMUNITY FAMILIES

DATE	FAMILY	PRAYER

COMMUNITY FAMILIES

DATE	FAMILY	PRAYER

COMMUNITY FAMILIES

DATE	FAMILY	PRAYER

COMMUNITY FAMILIES

DATE	FAMILY	PRAYER

COMMUNITY FAMILIES

DATE	FAMILY	PRAYER

COMMUNITY FAMILIES

DATE	FAMILY	PRAYER

COMMUNITY SCHOOLS

DATE	SCHOOL	PRAYER

COMMUNITY SCHOOLS

DATE	SCHOOL	PRAYER

COMMUNITY SCHOOLS

DATE	SCHOOL	PRAYER

COMMUNITY SCHOOLS

DATE	SCHOOL	PRAYER

COMMUNITY SCHOOLS

DATE	SCHOOL	PRAYER

COMMUNITY SCHOOLS

DATE	SCHOOL	PRAYER

COMMUNITY SCHOOLS

DATE SCHOOL PRAYER

COMMUNITY SCHOOLS

DATE	SCHOOL	PRAYER

COMMUNITY SCHOOLS

DATE	SCHOOL	PRAYER

COMMUNITY SCHOOLS

DATE	SCHOOL	PRAYER

COMMUNITY ORGANIZATIONS

DATE	ORG	PRAYER

COMMUNITY ORGANIZATIONS

DATE	ORG	PRAYER

COMMUNITY ORGANIZATIONS

DATE	ORG	PRAYER

COMMUNITY ORGANIZATIONS

DATE ORG PRAYER

COMMUNITY ORGANIZATIONS

DATE	ORG	PRAYER

COMMUNITY ORGANIZATIONS

DATE	ORG	PRAYER

COMMUNITY ORGANIZATIONS

DATE	ORG	PRAYER

COMMUNITY ORGANIZATIONS

DATE	ORG	PRAYER

COMMUNITY ORGANIZATIONS

DATE ORG PRAYER

COMMUNITY ORGANIZATIONS

DATE	ORG	PRAYER

MORE RESOURCES AVAILABLE

www.amazon.com/author/ericsanford

Eric Sanford is the founding pastor of Journeymen Church in Denver, CO. His passion is making disciples and teaching the Word of God. He has served as a youth pastor, church planter, pastor, and ministry coach. He is husband to Amanda and dad of Alex and Reagan.

Eric has created other journals designed to increase engagement with God and the Scriptures.

Made in the USA
Middletown, DE
18 October 2022

12972822R00086